Classical Me, Classical Thee

FOR
HOMESCHOOLERS

Classical Me, Classical Thee

FOR HOMESCHOOLERS

SQUANDER NOT THINE EDUCATION

Rebekah Merkle

canonpress

moscow, idaho | www.canonpress.com

Published by Canon Press
P.O. Box 8729, Moscow, Idaho 83843
800.488.2034 | www.canonpress.com

Cover and interior design by James Engerbretson.
Interior layout by Samuel Dickison.
Interior illustrations by James Engerbretson and Mark Beauchamp.

Printed in the United States of America.

Library of Congress Cataloging-in-Publication Data is forthcoming.

20 21 22 23   24 25 26 27 28   10 9 8 7 6 5 4 3 2 1

Of course, for Dad:
Some dads buy their kids ponies . . .
You cared more about giving us horsepower.

CONTENTS

If you have gone so far as to open the cover of this little book, then I think that you and I already have a lot in common.

You're a student being given a classical education.

Yeah—I did that too.

Although I wasn't homeschooled, I went all the way through a classical school, K-12, and I think I have a pretty fair idea of the kind of life you lead. I bet I know what kind of classes you have to take, what kind of books you have to read, and I bet I know what you think of them.

I might even understand some of your frustrations, your questions, and your boredom, as well as what intrigues you.

I decided to write this book because I have spent my entire life around students in your position. I went through a classical education and walked in your shoes myself; now my own kids are high school students being given a classical education, and they are currently walking in your shoes. I teach classes at a classical high school, so I spend every single day, eyeball to eyeball, with students who are jumping through the same hoops you're having to jump through. I have, in fact, seen the life of the classical student from pretty much every angle.

And let's face it. You're probably not doing the classical thing because *you* picked it.

I don't suppose that sometime in your early youth you sat down and read through a series of books discussing educational styles and decided that classical ed looked like the best option. It's possible that your parents may have done that with you ... but realistically, you're going through this because your parents were sold on the vision of classical education, not because you were.

This whole education thing is not something you chose; it's something that's being done to you. And when you were little, you never questioned it. But now that you're old enough to make a lot of your own choices in other areas (I'm assuming your mother doesn't still pick out your outfit every day), it may have occurred to you to wonder what the point of all this is. If you haven't asked the question out loud, you must have thought about it. Am I right? It probably went something like this:

In the middle of a gripping lesson on the uses of the Latin subjunctive, a voice inside your head says,

"What good is this ever going to do me in life?"

Perhaps you try to shush that voice and concentrate on your lesson – but it won't be shushed. A minute later it asks,

"Why on earth do I have to learn this?"

And if you ever ventured to voice these questions out loud, I'd be willing to bet that whatever answer you heard wasn't terribly compelling. Did someone tell you that Latin will help you with your English vocab and that you will be able to intuit the meanings of unusual words much more easily than other people?

('Yes," you think, "or I could just ask Siri and have a better answer in two seconds.")

Or perhaps they told you that if you go to med school you'll have a breeze of a time learning the names of medical conditions as opposed to all the other the unfortunate souls who never studied Latin?

("But I want to be a pilot," you mutter to yourself, "and chatting casually about the names of bacteria will—let us hope—NEVER be a part of my life.")

Maybe you were told that botanical names will be easier for you to decipher?

(Let's be real—that hardly seems like an alluring enough reason to have to study the subjunctive.)

Or possibly they mentioned that your math scores on standardized tests will be higher?

(And you sat there thinking that you don't even care enough about that statement to even formulate an opinion about it at all. Insert eye roll here.)

Or maybe they scolded you for having a bad attitude.

(And maybe you needed that and maybe you didn't.)

Or were you handed Dorothy Sayers' essay "The Lost Tools of Learning" to read?

Yeah, I'm sorry about that. **I'm assuming that you remain unconvinced, settled in skepticism, and counting the days until you can choose what college you go to, choose what major you want, and choose what classes you sign up for.**

Or maybe you're not that kid.

Maybe you're loyal to this whole project, you enjoy your classes, you like the books, and it really bugs you when your friends or siblings complain. But wouldn't you—even if you don't have a chip on your shoulder and a fuss in your voice—wouldn't you kind of like to hear the answers to those questions, too? Wouldn't it be helpful to know what the rationale is behind teaching you all this material? Wouldn't it be a bit handy to understand some of the behind-the-scenes decision-making which determined that you would learn this stuff? Because in my experience, even the most enthusiastic and on-board students still only have a very hazy notion of what all this is actually about.

Now, I do think there are some extremely compelling answers for this whole thing—I'm just not sure anyone has taken the time to actually spell them out for you.

Everyone's spending so much time giving you a classical education, it's possible that no one has taken the time to stop and tell you why they're doing it.

So here you go—I'm trying to take a shot at that.

Why bother with this? If you don't really have any choice in the matter and you're just going to be stuck in your school until you graduate, why bother reading about it? Why not just hunker down and get through it? Why not just start carving notches in the wall of your prison cell, marking the days until graduation and freedom? To answer that question, bear with me for a sec.

Let's say that you suddenly found out about the opportunity to be an intern on the film set of a major blockbuster movie that is going to be filmed in Italy this summer. You would get to spend your whole summer break on set, shadowing the director and getting a front-row seat watching how all this magic is being made. You would get a behind-the-scenes look at how everything works, from the actors to the special effects guys, the stunt men, the camera crews, the costume designers, and the editors. You could watch and learn from a world-class director as he weaves all that raw material into a gripping story. Let's say that you're interested in pursuing a career in film, and so not only will this whole experience be just plain fun, you also know that it would be of invaluable benefit to you as you get ready to start out on that career path. It could open any number of doors in the future, from what colleges you may attend to further film opportunities of the same kind. You know you would learn tons, and you know that you would come out of this experience with a huge head start over all the other kids who, just like you, are interested in pursuing a career in filmmaking.

Whether or not that particular scenario appeals to you, you can understand how it could appeal to someone. And furthermore, let's say that in order to get into this internship, you have to apply for it, you need to show exceptional talent and be highly qualified, you have to submit an original short film as part of the application process, and then you have to be selected out of thousands of other applicants who are all dying for the same thing. So you do it. You apply. You cross your fingers, you pray like crazy, and then ... against all the odds, you're selected.

You are actually the one lucky winner out of thousands who gets to go on this crazy ride.

With me so far? Now then. Once on the set in Italy, how are you going to feel about all the stuff the director is telling you about the whole process of filmmaking? You're standing in Rome outside the Colosseum in the late afternoon, helping set up the cameras, listening to the director explain how he wants to frame the shot and what he wants to capture as the actress runs across the street to catch a bus. He's talking about the light and why he's going to wait until the sun comes out from behind that cloud, and he's most insistent that the sunlight will profoundly affect the dramatic impact of the scene he's trying to create.

Let me ask you ... Are you groaning and rolling your eyes the whole time? Drumming your pencil on your notebook and dying a little bit inside? Asking yourself, or him, what is the point of it all? Wondering when this will possibly ever benefit you? Yawning ostentatiously, muttering "sheesh" under your breath at periodic intervals, and looking at your watch every two minutes?

Of course not. And the reason you wouldn't be doing that, is that you already value what it is that you're receiving. You know what a privilege it is. You know how crazy hard you had to work and how highly you had to achieve to be here. You see what an enormous opportunity it is. You see how great this is going to look on college applications. You know how this increases your chances of getting onto other sets in the future. Clearly you're not going to waste this moment by fussing, spacing off, or making the director wonder if he shouldn't just send you home. Obviously you're going to be giving this whole thing 110 percent of your effort and attention—and that's because when you value something, you treat it differently than you would if you thought it was worthless.

Now let me introduce you to another person along on this trip. Let's call him Logan. He's the nephew of one of the film crew, and he's stuck hanging out on the set in Italy with you all summer—which really bums him out because he wants to be skateboarding with his friends back home in Milwaukee, but he can't because his parents are forcing him to be on this stupid trip and it's totally lame and uncool. So he slumps around in the background with a tortured look on his face and spends the entire time staring at his phone. The two of you are receiving all the same opportunities, but you're getting two very different things out of it. Now, let's suppose that Logan finishes the summer, goes home to Milwaukee to pursue his dream of becoming a professional skateboarder, but things don't really go his way because it turns out that he's just not that good. So he enrolls in college and, after switching majors three or four times, he finally pulls himself together and fixes his attitude and realizes what it is he really wants to do ... pursue a career in filmmaking. And let's say this time around it really takes. Logan has figured out his passion—and it turns out that he's actually kinda talented at it.

Regardless of your thoughts on the internship, how do you think Logan feels when he looks back on that summer? Does he have any regrets? Might he wish that he had paid better attention? Would he wish that he could go back in time and change one or two or all of the details?

Many students from classical homeschools have wandered off into the sunset after graduation, and several years down the road have suddenly noticed how very useful their education is proving to be. **They value it now, but in retrospect—when it's quite a ways back in the rearview mirror.** Suddenly they look back at what they were given in high school, and they realize that they were handed something that very, very few people actually get. They suddenly see, in retrospect, that they lived through four years of exceptional opportunity that had all the potential to open ridiculous numbers of doors for them in their future career choices. Knowing now that it's valuable, they would treat it very differently if they had the chance to go back for a re-do. If they could travel back in time and take those same classes again, they would be much less like our friend Logan, and much more like our fictitious film intern. They'd be milking the moment for all it's worth—rather than just yawning through class, killing time staring blankly at the wall, and just waiting until college when they think that real life actually begins.

The truth is, real life doesn't begin in college. You're deep in it already.

The choices you're making right now drastically affect your actual life. And if you're being given a classical education, you're sitting in the midst of a huge pile of opportunities—but a lot of students haven't noticed them because they all seem so normal and humdrum. I would love for you homeschool students to realize what a crazy privilege you have, and understand how many people would kill to have received what you're yawning over. I think if you could pause for a moment and really grasp the significance of what you're receiving, it just might change the way you think about all the work you have to do every day. **And let's face it. You have to do the work anyway.** Wouldn't it be nice to find out that it's actually a huge (and very valuable) opportunity?

CHAPTER ONE

A Fundamentally Different Pizza

If you joined the classical bandwagon later on in your educational career, you probably have a decent idea of how a classical education is different from other models. But if you have gone all the way through (as I did) from kindergarten through high school, you might not actually know how very weird this whole thing is. It's easy to think, when you're surrounded by something all the time, that it's just what everybody does. You know. Rich kids think it's normal to spend Christmas break at their chalet in the Swiss Alps. Russian kids think it's normal to speak Russian. And you've spent a lot of time surrounded by siblings and friends who are also receiving a classical education, so you assume that the knowledge you're receiving is just basically a given. Yeah, you know that the public school kids don't have to learn Latin, and of course you realize that they don't have Bible class. But many students in your position just assume that they are receiving the same high school education as everyone else in America, but you're just doing it at home and there are some extra classes and maybe a few more old books thrown in to make it all seem a bit more swank.

Many classical students tend to think of high school as a giant Pizza Hut. All the American teen-agers are sitting at their various school tables eating pepperoni pizza, and meanwhile the classical home-schoolers are off on the side eating pepperoni with extra cheese and green peppers—but they also have to sit up straight and keep their napkins in their laps. Frequently, the students at the "classical education" tables look longingly across the room at everyone else, and wish they could sit out there in the middle too—it sure looks like they're having a lot more fun out there. Plus those kids don't have to eat the stupid green peppers.

Actually, though, that analogy doesn't work at all. You're sitting there eating your pizza, everyone else at your table is eating their pizza, and so you assume that's what the rest of the students around the

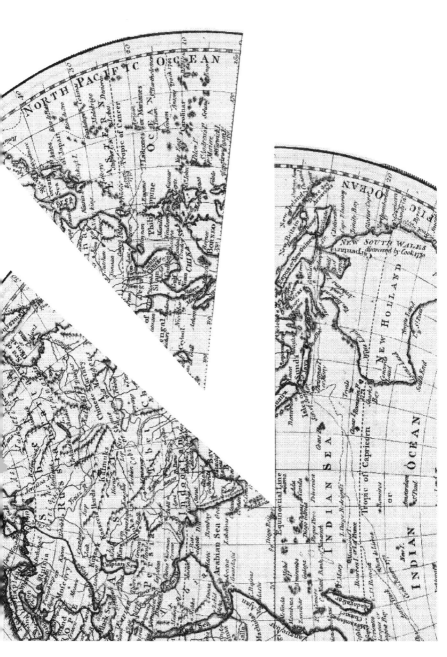

room are eating too. But if you were to actually go over there and sit down with them, you would discover they're being served something entirely different. This confusion will eventually be made evident to you at some point, if it hasn't been already. Take my word for it. One of these days you'll be sitting in a college class, and you'll contribute something to the discussion like, "Well you know how pepperoni pizza tastes ... " and you'll be surprised to find that the entire class has swiveled around and is looking at you like you just sprouted a second head before their very eyes. You try again, "You know—pepperoni? Anyone?" and they all look completely blank. At this point you're saying to yourself, "What the heck were they eating over there all that time? I could have sworn they had pepperoni on their pizzas ... " The truth is that they weren't eating pizza at all. They were over there having tuna and crackers that entire time, and they have absolutely no idea what you're even talking about.

This is because you're not just receiving a regular old generic-brand education with a few add-ons like Latin. You're being given something that's really and truly unique.

Your public school friends from youth group or the soccer team are receiving an education that is fundamentally different than yours.

So what's the difference then? What's the big deal? To answer that question I'm going to back up a little bit. I'm not going to talk about the importance of Latin (yet), and I'm not going to get into tedious topics like pedagogical methods and learning styles and developmental phases (at least not in detail). Those are all things that would be important to you if you were a teacher or a parent. But you're not that. Your mom and dad and any teachers you have are putting in a lot of time and effort, trying to turn you into something. However, the most pressing concern for you is not the techniques they are using ... you are probably more interested in what the end goal is. If you had a team of designers and engineers who were working on building a custom car for you, your biggest questions would be "What's it going to look like?" and "How fast will it drive?" You don't want to be told all the mathematical equations the engineers are using. That's their job, and it's interesting to them, and they talk about it amongst themselves on their lunch breaks, but that part doesn't really matter to you as much.

You want to know about the final product. Let's talk about that.

CHAPTER TWO

Puzzle Skills

So what is everyone trying to turn you into? This is pretty simple, actually. The various people involved with your education, from your parents to your co-op or online teachers, are all trying to work together to turn you into a leader. They want you to become the kind of person who rises to the top like cream, the kind of person that others will instinctively follow, the kind of person who stands out from the crowd. **They don't want to work on transforming you into an unquestioning little cog in the machine, a drone for the hive, an unremarkable face in the crowd.** They want to see you out in front, making a difference, effecting change. But that, of course, is only half the battle. It's no good being a leader if you have no idea where you're going or why. A leader with a crowd behind him, wandering around with no clear direction, is not exactly a win.

A few years from now, as you sit in a college classroom, we hope that your professors and your classmates will notice there's something different about you. But, believe it or not, we aren't hoping that you will stand out because of your IQ or your SAT scores.

What we want others to be struck by is the fact that you actually know what you think and why you think it.

We want them to be surprised by the fact that you're confident in your opinions, and you don't mind defending them against all comers. We want them to see that you are a person whose opinions are actually all consistent with each other, that you defend your political opinions, for example, with the same reasoning that you use to defend your philosophical and artistic and historical and literary opinions. In fact, we want them to see you arguing for your political opin-

ions based on your historical opinions. Or arguing for your artistic opinions based on your philosophical opinions. We want them to see you argue about history from literature, or about literature from art, and all without really changing the subject. We want them to see you evaluate all the new information you'll be receiving, sift it, reject some of it, keep some of it, and fit what you keep into your already existing frame of knowledge. This is much more rare a skill than you may realize. And, when someone possesses it, they immediately stand out from the crowd.

Imagine that you've been handed a puzzle box, and your job is to complete the puzzle. It's one of those difficult ones with zillions of pieces, but the bad news is that the box also contains pieces from three different puzzles, which have all been mixed up together. Your job is to complete the puzzle that goes with the box. Obviously your first step is to set up the box right there in front of you, and as you pick up each piece, to try and decide whether it belongs in this puzzle or not. The way you tell if it does is by comparing it to the picture on the box. The project is complicated, yes, but certainly not impossible. Now imagine that you had the same task, only this time you didn't have the box to look at. What was originally a difficult project has now become a hopelessly complicated project, as I'm sure you can imagine. If someone takes away your box, you're basically reduced to picking up pieces at random and checking to see if they fit with one another. At some point you would just stop trying, assuming that none of them fit anyway, so who cares? You would probably end by dumping them all into a drawer and walking away.

Every human in this world is confronted with the puzzle pieces in the form of competing facts, claims, evidence, and opinions.

These bombard us all day long and from every angle. No one is free from this, but some have been equipped to handle the bombardment more effectively than others. If you have been given a classical Christian education, you have been handed the box with the picture on the front. In fact, you spend all day, every day, studying that box, being shown various objects of interest, being forced to notice this detail or that one, being shown that this neon pink piece you're staring at couldn't possibly fit into this picture anywhere so you should set it aside, being made to notice that shadow under the tree over there on the left, etc. You spend your days being given a framework, a means by which you can evaluate whatever piece is currently in front of you. When you study literature you're staring at one set of pieces, when you switch to math you're looking at others, but in the end all the pieces are forming different parts of the same picture. This is what everyone is going on about when they talk about a cohesive worldview.

When you go away to college, when you enter the workforce, for the rest of your life in fact, you will be learning new things. Each new fact that comes your way is another puzzle piece—one that you've never seen before. But if you know what the picture on the box is, and you remember how to look at a piece and compare it to that picture, you'll be able to fit that piece in where it is supposed to go, or reject it because you know that it doesn't belong.

This is not rocket science, and being able to do it is a very basic skill. But to someone who has never seen the picture on the box, who doesn't know that there even is a box, to someone who has a lot of disconnected pieces in front of him, your ability to evaluate and fit the pieces together will seem very nearly superhuman. The modern public education system in America has made a very focused effort to throw away the box and make sure none of the students ever see it. The poor students (none of whom are responsible for the situation, by the way) spend their days bombarded with facts, with things to memorize, with more pieces of various puzzles, but none of it hangs together because the modern educational establishment is actually at war with the very idea of a box. **They believe in a random universe which arrived here through blind chance—and in that worldview nothing coheres. Students memorize stuff, but no one expects it to connect.**

It's not that the classical method teaches the students more facts than the public schools do, although that's frequently true. It's not that the classical method teach different facts than the public schools, although that's often true too. The biggest and most fundamental difference between what you are receiving and what the rest of American teenagers are receiving is that **you are being taught to look at life as if it makes sense, as if it all hangs together and is all part of the same picture.** You're being taught to think about it critically. You are not just being given lists of facts to memorize before the test on Friday after which point you can safely forget them. The most vital thing that you are being taught is not the facts themselves, it is the skill of being able to analyze them.

You may not ever have heard this from a responsible adult before, but here goes.

You will forget facts.

Let's face it, I have no idea what books I even read in ninth grade, much less am I able to tell you the years in which they were written or where the authors were born. And you know what? That's ok. If I ever need to know who wrote *The Bridge of San Luis Rey*, I will look it up and find out. Worst-case scenario, I can always read it again. But the skills that I learned in those lit classes are skills that have stuck with me, skills that I have used every time I've watched a movie or seen a TV show or listened to a song on the radio. In my high school lit classes, I learned how to think about and evaluate stories, how to pick apart what they are saying and assess whether it's true, and I still know how to do that even though I forgot what on earth *The Bridge of San Luis Rey* is even about. (Did a bridge fall down? Maybe? Or possibly everyone was just worried that it would?)

So the takeaway truth is that you're learning skills, not just facts. You're probably way too young to have seen or cared about the movie *The Karate Kid* (although they probably have a remake or three by now). Anyway, in that film the boy hopes to become good at karate, and his teacher, instead of teaching him to fight, annoyingly makes him do a bunch of chores. He has to paint the fence, he has to sand the decks, and he has to wax the car, lots of times. It all seems tedious and boring and uninteresting and not at all what he wants to be doing ... but of course there comes a moment in the movie when he discovers that he wasn't just doing chores at all, he was learning moves. The moves were becoming ingrained in him until they were instinctive—and it turns out that

Mr. Miyagi was teaching him how to fight after all. And that's what your classes are like. Your parents are not making you memorize facts because someday when you're thirty-four years old your boss might suddenly give you a pop quiz on the major dates of the Wars of the Roses. Instead, they're making you paint the fence, and the skills that you learn will stick with you long after the facts themselves have gotten hazy.

However, comma. Those skills will only stick with you if you are, in fact, learning the skills. **It is possible to approach even a classical education in a way that ensures you will get nothing terribly profound out of it.** Go back to the puzzle analogy. Let's say that you really don't see what the big deal is about the box. All you care about is your grade, so you diligently ask,

"Will this be on the test?"

and you make sure to click your pieces together when you're told to. But you never pay attention to the box because you don't see the point. When you graduate and head out into the world, you may have a little bit of an advantage over other kids, but not for long. **From graduation onward you will have no idea whatsoever about where to put anything ... because you were focused on the individual pieces, not the overall picture. The facts without the skills.**

Everyone involved in giving you this education wants to see you turned into a leader, and they think that the classical method is the best way to achieve that. So what is it about a classical education that makes them think that?

CHAPTER THREE

The Right Map

Let's say that you are in Chicago, and you're about to start a road trip to New York City. You know that's where you want to end up, although you're not super clear about which direction it is from your hotel. But you've expertly loaded up your car, and you're driving toward the Chicago city limits, after which point you figure you'll just drive down the road and eventually fetch up in New York. You had a friend who drove to New York and arrived successfully, so you know it can be done, and why wouldn't it work in your case as well? In one way, getting to the Big Apple from the Windy City truly *is* as simple as driving down the road—but in another sense there are thousands of ways to do it wrong. You could head south and find yourself in Mexico, you could head west and wash up in LA, you could veer to the southeast and end up in Florida. Your master plan of "driving down the road" will work, but obviously that's only the case if you have managed to pick the right road. The happy news, though, is that there are such things as maps in the world. You don't have to flip a coin every time you come to an intersection.

You can actually follow the map.

In the same way that not every road leads to New York City, not every educational path leads to the same end product of faithful, clear-thinking, creative, persuasive leaders. Millions and millions of American teenagers are being given mandatory educations, and, to put it mildly, not all of them are turning out to be clear-thinking leaders. But you're doing this the way your are because someone, somewhere, wants you to be that different kind of person—articulate, creative, clear-thinking, and persuasive—and they think classical Christian education is the most effective road to get you there. They've looked at the map, they've charted the route, and they've put you on this road.

Why do they think that? If the desired result is for you to be a strong, persuasive, independent shaper of culture, what is it about your school that makes it the best road towards that objective? What is it about the classical method that produces leaders? Aren't leaders just people who happen to have been born with strong personalities? Well, no, actually. Your natural personality is a hugely important part of who you will become, but it is your personality as much as your intellect that is being shaped through your education. A naturally bubbly, extroverted girl can be made, by her education, to be insecure, embarrassed, and ill-equipped for life, just as a naturally shy girl can be made, by her education, much more confident and sure of herself. In both cases her natural personality has been molded by her education.

In the next chapters, let's look at some of the goals of your education and then compare them with the means by which everyone thinks you can get there.

First of all, we all hope that, at the end of this educational process, you will be able to think clearly. Presumably, you wish that too. Thinking clearly seems obvious enough, but you would be amazed at how atypical a skill it actually is. The ability to work through an issue clearly, logically, and precisely is an exceptionally rare gift that you are being given.

Something similar goes on in sports, but for some reason it's much easier for people to see the principle there than in the classroom. Everyone recognizes that when a coach makes his basketball team run suicides or do box jumps, **he is training them for something else.** When he makes the team do shooting drills, it is so that once they are in a game, they will possess the necessary skills needed to win the game. No one thinks that the dribbling drills are the end goal of the basketball season, or that you need to do box jumps because sometimes in the middle of the game there is a box-jumping competition you'll have to win. Practices are all about deconstructing the necessary skills for a basketball game, isolating them, and then working on them individually ... but always with a larger goal in mind.

Each basketball game is different from the last one you played. That's true even if you're playing against the same team. Every time you dribble down the court, you are faced with a unique set of challenges. You have never seen this exact situation before, but the skills your coach spent all that time drilling into you turn out to have been useful after all, which you will appreciate when you find yourself able to instinctively drive past the other team's defense for a layup.

For some reason, people don't realize that the same thing is true in the classroom.

The facts you are being taught are not the end goal of learning any more than the wall sit is the end goal of basketball.

You are spending your days in the classroom doing drills in much the same way that you do in basketball practice. They are all designed to equip you, to strengthen you, to make you into a person who can step out of the classroom and into the world and successfully negotiate situations you have never encountered before.

Let's say there is a hypothetical member of your basketball team who has set himself up as a skeptic. When the team is doing weight training, he points out that he's never seen anyone in the whole history of basketball have to bench-press during a game. Nor has he seen anyone do a sit-up. Or run a suicide. He therefore declines to do any of those things in practice. I think we can all predict what kind of basketball player that boy will be. In the same way, it is entirely possible to sit through a classical education but come out the other side with precisely none of the skills which it was designed to impart. **And if that's the way you approach your education, then you are basically making the decision now that you would like to be the person who, throughout the rest of his life, sits on the bench and watches the actual players.**

Hopefully your basketball coach would be able to answer your questions if you said, "Hey—how do suicides help our performance in games?" In the same way, your educators hopefully know the answers to how your classroom work is supposed to help you in life. But often they can't be bothered to talk about that, because they're too busy making you do the work to pause and explain the big picture. So I'll do my best to answer your questions here.

CHAPTER FOUR

Behind the Drill: Latin

Let's deconstruct the drills a bit. I'm going to pick a few of the basic classes and typical assignments that you likely face on a daily basis and try to give you a "behind the scenes" look at why they matter and why they're actually worth your time.

We'll start here, because Latin is one of the most obvious features of a classical education and possibly one that chaps your hide more than other things. It's also likely something you have to explain to people. Now that classical brick-and-mortar schools and homeschools are decently common, people are getting a bit more used to the idea of Latin, but I'm sure you've had to answer questions from random uncles at Thanksgiving:

"Why on earth are they making you learn Latin? Who do they think you're going to talk to— the Pope?!"

And then you smile weakly and say something smart like, "Haha, right?" Or perhaps they cheerily quote, "Latin is a dead, dead language, / dead as dead can be,/ it killed the ancient Romans, / and it's slowly killing me." (How is it that everyone knows that ditty?) No one ever responds this way to kids who take science or math classes, or even when they hear you are taking Spanish. But Latin magically brings out the skeptic in many people.

First, we need to discuss language in general. Language is actually much more profound than it seems like it should be. Starting at the beginning with creation, how exactly was it that God made the world? He spoke it into existence. He used words—or rather The Word, which we find out (in John) is actually Christ. Christ is the Word of God who was with Him in the beginning. God shaped our universe through His Word, and then He gave Adam his first job, which happened to be to name the animals. So God created using language—His language which was actually Himself—and then He assigned Adam to bestow names—even more words—on that creation. God designed humans to speak, and to take dominion over His creation in part by how we speak about it. When we name things or discover the names for things, we are mimicking God's creativity. And, oddly enough, it shapes us when we do it. When we learn a new word, it actually brings clarity to our minds in a weird way. It's not just handy to have the correct label for things so that we know how to say, "Please pass the mustard" instead of pointing and grunting.

Here's an example: Imagine for a second that you didn't know what the word *déjà vu* meant, and you'd never heard it before. Let's further imagine that you experienced *déjà vu* on a regular basis. You were frequently just going innocently along through the day and suddenly getting weird feelings that you'd done this before. You'd look around confused for a second, then the feeling would pass, and everything would be normal again. Imagine how unsettling that would be if you didn't know what it was! But then say you explained the sensation to someone who said, "Oh yeah—that's *déjà vu*." Suddenly it's not as unsettling anymore—you have a handle for it. A peg to hang it on in your mind. The next time it happens, you know exactly what to call it—and this is a much more reassuring feeling than not knowing what it is. And notice that the reassurance doesn't come from knowing the scientific explanation for how *déjà vu* happens. It simply comes from knowing the word.

Here's a new word that you probably don't know, but I guarantee you have experienced. Have you ever been completely embarrassed, mortified, ashamed, and humiliated by something that your friend or your little brother is doing? Basically, he's the one who should be embarrassed—but for some reason he isn't—and all the embarrassment lands on you and you're not even the one doing it? As a kid I remember getting this feeling during talent shows when the person on the stage should definitely not have been on the stage—yet they didn't seem to notice. They proceeded merrily along with their squeaky trumpet playing, feeling very pleased with themselves, and meanwhile I was ready to slide under my seat in vicarious embarrassment for them. The Germans actually have a word for this. It's *fremdschämen*—the sensation of being ashamed for someone else. Somehow when you learn the word, it suddenly crystallizes the sensation. Clarity has just been brought to the situation. Now, the next time your mom is singing loudly along to the 80s radio station when your friends are in the car, you'll have a word for it. You'll recognize the sensation, even if you don't remember what that German word was. Reading about it has made you stop for a moment and analyze that feeling—and now it's hanging on a neat little hook in your brain because we've given it a label.

As you expand your vocabulary, you're learning much more than lists of words. You're learning about the universe.

You're parsing feelings, sensations, actions, categories ... You are broadening your mind. **This is why studying foreign languages is so good—it expands the benefit of vocabulary study exponentially.** This is because other languages often describe things slightly differently than we do, and this teaches us to see the universe more broadly. This may be one of those urban legends, but I've often heard that Eskimos have sixteen (or thirty-six or something) different words for snow. I don't know if that's true, but it seems likely enough. How many words do I have for snow? I can think of six: *snow, slush, sleet, hail, powder,* and *corn snow.* Each of those categories is just a bit different from the others, but if you live in a part of the country without snow, then you probably don't even know all of those.

But what if an Eskimo spent the winter here in Idaho and taught me more than just the words I already know? I would actually really love that—because sometimes the snow comes down in enormous wet glops, and other times it's flurries of tiny flakes. Sometimes the snow is so cold it squeaks when you walk on it, and sometimes it's lumpy, and sometimes it's sparkly. Sometimes the wind blows the snow off the tree branches and all of the air glitters when the sun is out, and I have no idea what to call it when that happens. If I had forty-two different words for snow, then I think I would actually notice the snow more than I do. I wouldn't just call all of it "snow"—I would get to use the right word. And that would make me look just a little bit more closely at God's creation.

Having a word for something makes us see that something more clearly.

"OK, fine," you say. "But why Latin? I would much rather learn French, because I want to travel during college and Paris sounds fun. And no matter where I travel I'm not going to bump into a Roman centurion and have to ask him for directions." Yes, that's true. And yes, modern languages do actually provide the same benefits I've just described as far as vocabulary is concerned. But there's more than just vocabulary building going on when you study another language. There's also the structure of the language—how the words are put together. And in just the same way that the right word brings greater clarity to your thoughts, so does sentence structure.

Let me ask you a question—and hopefully if you've studied Latin and paid attention at all, you'll be able to answer it.

What is the difference between these two sentences: "He was running" and "He ran"? Think about that for a second and see if you can articulate the difference. Assuming your Latin is relatively fresh, you will recognize that the first sentence is in the imperfect tense and the second is in the perfect. What is the difference between those two? The first sentence has ongoing action in the past, the second has completed action in the past. I'm guessing that you came up with some version of that as your answer. But if I stopped some random English speaker on the street and surprised them with that question, they would have a very hard time answering it. They intuitively know there is a difference inasmuch as they recognize that those are sentences they would use themselves—but they wouldn't be able to answer the question, because they've never had to stop and think about it before. You have. That means that you understand with greater precision how to use the English language because you bring that greater understanding back with you from Latin. It's basically putting a sharper edge on your blade. And Latin is absolutely terrific at doing this because it is an incredibly methodical language. It's very predictable and very structured and extremely specific—and this means that it provides that mental sharpening unbelievably well.

Of course there are also the huge facts that Latin was the language of our heritage in the West, the language of Christendom for a millennia, and one of the parent languages of English. If you want to learn any modern Romance language eventually (say, if you really do want to travel to Paris in college), you will find that Latin is an excellent foundation to build upon. But I'm sure you've heard all of those reasons already. I'm just hoping to convince you that—even if you forget all the Latin chants you've ever had to memorize and you never go on to learn any other languages—your mind has already been shaped, expanded, and sharpened by your study of Latin, even if you haven't noticed it happening. Your use of English—and therefore the use of your mind—is more precise and more accurate than it otherwise would be as a result of your Latin experience. I know it's easy to think that English is something that is bestowed equally upon all native speakers, but that is just flat-out not the case. If you don't believe me, I would simply ask you to ponder the excellence of craft in the average comment under a YouTube video, and then get back to me on coherent and clear English being natural to all speakers. In fact, to prove my point, I have just pulled up YouTube and found what seems to be an instructional home-improvement video. Beneath it, my eye lit upon this comment, and I promise you I did not spend any time at all trying to find something ridiculous. This is

een someone be
s pulling vinyl
when u fold
u should dog
ling back from
t you could tear
cheap or if
s Like this guy

POST

after a two-second google:

> *"I've never seen someone be that careless pulling vinyl back to glue when u fold back to glue u should dog ear when pulling back from under cabinet you could tear vinyl if it's cheap or if your careless Like this guy"*

Hmm. I'm unclear as to what he's trying to tell us. I gather that he disapproves of the methods displayed in the video, but beyond that it's more than a bit hazy and vague. So. The ability to accurately articulate a thought is not an inherent gift. You, on the other hand, are being forced to concentrate on language itself, on how it fits together, on how you can take a thought or a sentiment and then translate it accurately into different words. This is just like doing shooting drills in basketball—after a while it begins to pay off with your ability to drain shots on a regular basis. And, hopefully, after all this language training, if you decided to speak your mind on how vinyl should be glued to a floor, you would be able to do so in a crystal clear fashion, and the Internet would not be left in any doubt regarding what you were trying to say.

Take these sentences:

1. You will give me ten dollars.
2. You should give me ten dollars.
3. Give me ten dollars.

There are subtle distinctions between those three sentences, but they make all the difference as to the meaning, right? But you have had to spend time in your Latin exercises running analysis on what exactly the difference is between them (indicative versus subjunctive versus imperative) and figuring out how you would represent that difference precisely in another language. **When you come out the other end of the chute after years of this, you will have a brain that is more organized, discerning, attuned to nuance, and capable of saying exactly what you want to say ... and (this is the most important part) your mind will have been trained to do that even if you forget all the Latin you ever studied.**

CHAPTER FIVE

Behind the Drill: Literature

On the Latin question, it's quite easy to see the difference between what you are getting and what the average American high schooler is getting. You have to learn Latin, they don't. But what about subjects like literature? Surely you're getting the same basic stuff when it comes to lit, right? Maybe you have to read more "classics" than average high school students do, but they've read more modern "greats." Beyond the actual book list, what differences could there possibly be?

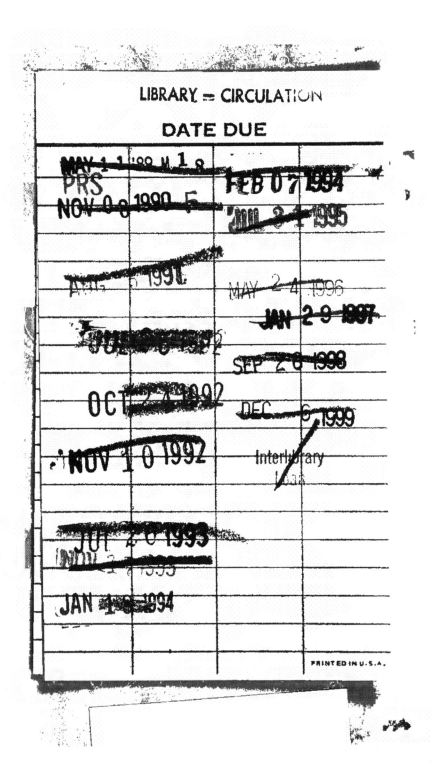

Huge differences, I'm afraid. You are developing skills in lit class that are going to serve you incredibly well in your future life and are going to make you stand out from the crowd—but you may actually have no idea that your old lit class was where you learned them.

Let's say that you are assigned to read a short story. So you muscle through it, you pay attention, and then you will probably have to answer some questions about it. Maybe a quiz, maybe a discussion, maybe an essay, maybe something else. But someone expects that you did actually read the material, you figured out what it was talking about, and you can then answer basic factual questions about it. So far this seems pretty obvious. But here's where the magic happens. You are being taught to answer the question,

"What does it mean?"

and that is a fundamentally different question than

"What does it mean to you?"

Think about that for a second. If you ask the question, "What does it mean?" you are having to analyze what the author was trying to say. But if you ask the question, "What does it mean to you?" then you are basically saying, "What thoughts were in your head as you read this short story? What did it remind you of?" And of course, there are no wrong answers to that question.

"What does it mean?" presupposes that there are right and wrong answers. If you happen to be thinking about Easter bunnies while you were reading an Edgar Allen Poe story, that doesn't necessarily mean that bunnies have anything whatsoever to do with what Poe was trying to say.

To be honest, this is actually an area where Christians tend to do well, even if they haven't been classically educated. This is because Christians are students of the Word, and we read our Bibles and assume we need to figure out what it's saying. The basics of junior high Bible study end up serving us very well.

I assume you've all been in a Bible class or a Bible study which goes something like this: The teacher has you all open up your Bibles to Luke 4 and read the following verse: "And he came to Nazareth, where he had been brought up. And as was his custom, he went to the synagogue on the Sabbath day, and he stood up to read."

Then your teacher says, "What town is Jesus in now?" and the whole group of junior high students stare at him blankly. He asks again, "What town is this?" After a long, awkward pause, eventually someone volunteers the answer, *"Jesus."*

"No," the teacher answers, "look at the verse. What does it say?" The kid tries again, *"God?"* Eventually, after much agony, the teacher succeeds in getting the students to look at the actual verse instead of staring at his forehead. Once they do this, someone finally figures out the right answer. *"Nazareth?"*

I know this seems absurd, but as you graduate and head off to college and into the workplace, your ability to answer basic factual questions about what someone else is saying—whether they are saying it in person or in print—will actually seem to many other people, as I've said, like a superpower.

I'm not even kidding. Our modern educational system has focused so much on the question "What does this mean to you?" and has insisted for so long that there are no wrong answers to this question that many people are absolutely unable to discern the difference between another person's actual words and "thoughts I was thinking in my head while you were talking." It's like a word-association game run horribly amok. In our family we have a car game called "Toodleyboogles" which majors on this exact thing. I say "crayon" and the next person says "blue." Then it's on to the next person who says "ocean," and by the end of the game you have worked your way from "crayon" to "streptococcus." As a time waster, it's kinda fun, but as an academic exercise, it's dreadful. This is the fundamental difference between rigorous study and the lit crit that is taught in most schools.

Like I said, Christians do tend to have a head start on developing this skill simply due to the basic exercise of Bible study. *What does the verse say?* Most of us are used to the idea that there is a right and wrong answer to that question. But your classical school is training you to examine all works of literature in a similar way. Obviously you don't treat every book as if it was inspired by God, but you assume that the author had something particular in mind when he wrote, and your job is to find out what that is. It's not your job to pontificate on whatever daydreams you were having as you read the book.

Let me offer another example. My husband got his doctorate at Oxford University, and while we were there, he took a number of classes with people who were insanely smart. Pick-up-a-new-language-in-six-months smart. Remember-every-fact-they-ever-heard smart. But he had one impressive ninja skill which frequently had the whole class amazed at his intellect—he was able to say, "I think Jesus was in Nazareth at this point." I'm not making this up. They would read something as a group (generally a sixteenth-century manuscript of some sort), and then they would all struggle to find the meaning. Various people would offer absurd suggestions, and eventually when he would volunteer what seemed like a totally obvious answer, they would all be blown away by his profound observation. The ability to look at a text and answer a question from it—that's an astonishing superpower. I know this seems silly and exaggerated and you probably don't believe me, but that's because you've been forced to do this over and over so many times that it seems very humdrum. But in order to answer the question "What does it mean?" you have to exert some self-discipline.

You have to set aside your own thoughts and force yourself to follow the argument and be able to discern the difference between what the author wrote and what you would prefer to be thinking about.

Many people have never actually had to do that—and it leaves them woefully unprepared to deal with life.

CHAPTER SIX

Behind the Drill: Logic

One of the other distinctives of classical education is the study of formal logic. You likely went through this in junior high or thereabouts. Once again, this is one of those mind-shaping exercises that you probably take completely for granted. I mean, logic seems so obvious, right? For instance, I'm betting you would throw a penalty flag if I tried to say this to you:

> *If aliens had kidnapped you and then wiped your memory, you wouldn't remember anything about it afterwards. You don't remember being kidnapped by aliens? That obviously proves you have been!*

That seems to be such a flawed bit of reasoning work that it feels like no one in their right mind could possibly fall for it. But what if I give you an example of the same thing, but one that didn't involve aliens:

> *If you flake out in school and don't pay any atten-*
> *tion and don't care about your grades and never*
> *do your homework, then you'll perform badly on*
> *your tests. You just bombed this test—which obvi-*
> *ously means you haven't paid any attention, you*
> *don't care about your grades, and you never did*
> *any homework.*

Hopefully you would recognize that this isn't simply an unjust (I hope!) accusation, but it's also logically flawed. If you're really on your logic game, then you'll notice that in both sample arguments I have been sneakily and nefariously affirming the consequent. Because of course there could be heaps of reasons you bombed the test, possibly up to and including you having been kidnapped by aliens and having your memory wiped.

My point here, though, is that you have been trained to watch for shoddy logic. I hope you apply this skill across the board and not just in your 8th grade logic exercises. When someone with a great smile and nice hair says something bonkers and tries to sell you something—whether it's an idea or a product—hopefully you are able to actually listen to what they're saying, see past the smile, and quietly resolve to not give this person your money or your loyalty or your vote, or whatever.

Unfortunately many grown people in America couldn't think their way out of a paper bag. They can't connect one thought to another because they've never been shown how to do it, and this means they will fall for all kinds of nonsense. They are like a person with no immune system—they'll catch whatever bug is going around.

Life is like a poker game you have to play.

(Work with me here.)

And some of the people sitting at the table with you are cheating in all kinds of ways.

They have aces up their sleeves, they've got someone feeding them information, they've rigged the deck, strategically placed mirrors, whatever. **If you play the game by their rules, then I guarantee you will get taken to the cleaners.** But let's say that you've been trained to spot cheating when it happens. You see the card being dealt from the bottom of the deck and are able to stop the game. Do you see what an enormous advantage that would give you? If you have been taught how to look for and identify cheating, then you have a much better chance in that game than the poor schmuck who doesn't even know that cheating is a possibility.

That's what your study of logic has been. You've been taught what cheating looks like in a line of argument, you've been taught how to spot it, and hopefully you'll become the kind of person who doesn't fall for it. Your classical education is a lot like self defense. In the marketplace of ideas there are many people who are going to try to mug you—and everyone involved in your education is trying to give you the necessary skills to fight them off. Some of the people want your actual money, and they'll try to sell you things with all kinds of dubious sales pitches. Other people want your loyalty to a cause, whether social or political or religious. You are already being deluged on Facebook and Instagram and Snapchat and in movies and music and TV shows with all sorts of claims and arguments and ideas—and we classical educators want you to be a hard sell. We want you to be the kind of person who is impossible to sneak up on.

When the Disney princess or Beyoncé tells you to follow your heart because it will never lead you astray, we want you to look at that claim with a steely gaze and examine it for flaws.

We want you to flip it over and look for hidden assumptions. When the Facebook ad shows you photos of all the horrible things that will happen to your digestive track if you don't instantly order the Secret Elixir of the Ancient Pharaohs, we don't want you to immediately get out your credit card. When the politician promises you that, if elected, he will ensure you have free chocolate milk forever, we want you to double-check the facts.

It is possible, though, to learn logic and then steadfastly refuse to apply it to your life. It's possible to tuck that knowledge away in its own compartment, treat it like a contagious disease, and never let it come into contact with your decision-making process. This is what I was talking about at the beginning of this book. It's entirely possible for students to sit through the classes, tick the boxes, do the exercises, earn the A on the transcript, and then dust off their hands and leave it all behind forever. Your logic book can get you to memorize fallacies, but it can't force you to let that knowledge affect your life.

Not to flatter you too much, but you're the horse who is being led to water—but they can't make you drink. That part is up to you.

CHAPTER SEVEN

Behind the Drill: Rhetoric

Another class you *must* take that is unique to classical schools is rhetoric. If you mentioned your rhetoric homework to your cousin who goes to the public high school, the likely response would be, "What on earth is rhetoric?" and then maybe you would smugly rattle off Aristotle's definition of rhetoric that you had to memorize, or maybe you would roll your eyes and make an uncouth noise in the back of your throat to make it clear that rhetoric is a giant waste of your time. (It's hard to say because I don't know which particular variety of classical high school student you are.)

Let's go with the first answer for starters. Let's say that **you are the kind of kid who wears his pants way too high and purses his lips and looks sternly at people and corrects their grammar** and who is just waiting for the moment when he can rattle off a bit of Aristotle to wow his audience. You like to think of yourself as the picture-perfect example of the ideal classical student. If that's you, then the sad and painful truth is that you have no idea what rhetoric is about—despite the fact that you may have memorized all the definitions and could beat absolutely anyone in a race to identify the *narratio* and outline the *refutatio*. You're exactly like the kid who learned the logical fallacies as if they were foreign vocabulary words that he had to know for the test but who is fundamentally unable to actually spot a fallacy in the wild.

"How so?" you may be indignantly asking, hiking your pleated pants up a little higher and exposing the white socks above your penny loafers. Well, because you're doing it all wrong. A successful rhetorician is not one who knows how to recite definitions—he's one who knows how to persuade people and make them want to listen to him. I prefer Plato's definition of rhetoric over Aristotle's anyway, and he says that rhetoric is the "art of enchanting the soul." And if you think that you are enchanting the soul of your public school cousin by pompously reciting Aristotle at him,* then you haven't even gotten to the first introductory step of successful rhetoric.

But what if you're not that kid. You sneer at that kid. You wouldn't be caught dead in a ditch with that kid. When your cousin asks you what rhetoric is, you register utter contempt and make it clear that you are far too cool to be tainted by these embarrassing things your education is trying to do to you. Your head is bloody but unbowed. You may be forced to take rhetoric, but you have remained resolutely, staunchly cool. You will not succumb to the torture. You make dismissive noises about the whole subject, and you never, *ever* wear your pants too high. Well, you're not winning either, I'm afraid, and that's because you're not actually persuading anyone of anything except of the fact that you're not a leader—you're a follower. **Whatever the cool police say to do, you hop to and do it. You're being led around by the (very cool) ring in your (very cool) nose, and you are (very) far from being someone who influences and persuades.** You may have a loyal group of fans who affirm your every hairdo, but that's because they are groupies who were just like you already, and already had all the same loyalties to "the cool" that you do.

A leader is someone who can change people's minds, who is compelling enough that others want to

*Aristotle's definition of rhetoric is, of course, "the faculty of observing, in any given case, the available means of persuasion." Aristotle may have worn pleated high-waisters, as well.

follow. A leader makes people want to step out from wherever they were in order to come across and fall into step.

Rhetoric is the class that's trying to turn you into a leader.

You can resist if you want, but that's what it's there for. You're being taught how to persuade—and it's just an obvious fact that persuasive people end up at the front of the pack. Maybe that seems dull and boring and stupid—but only to someone who isn't interested in leading and only wants to follow.

But what if you have no interest in becoming a world leader? You don't want to be a dictator or a congressman, so what's the point? Let's say that you want to become a realtor and sell houses to people. Well, let's think about that for a second. Do you think that "being persuasive" could be of value in that profession?

OK, no, so you don't want to be a realtor—you want to start your own bakery and sell French pastries. You want to deal exclusively with butter and eggs and flour, and you have no interest in being a "leader." Well, would you prefer to have it be a successful bakery, or a flop of a bakery? Do you think it might

be helpful to know how to write irresistible pitches for investors—something that makes them want to plunk their money down to back your fabulous, floury idea? Would it be good to know how to write advertising copy that makes people want to come visit? Would it be beneficial to be able to create a website that makes people stop everything they're doing and immediately drive down to your new pâtisserie to try out your croissants? That's what rhetoric is for. It's there to help you sell your pastries. It's the reason when you and your fellow microbiologists have worked through the research, and now it's time to present your findings at a conference, they all look over at you and say, "You do it—you speak well."

I said at the beginning that the people involved in giving you this education want you to rise to the top like cream after you graduate and leave—and rhetoric is the class that is teaching you how to rise to the top, now that some of the necessary groundwork has been laid. It may not seem like it's teaching you those practical skills now. I'm fairly confident that you haven't talked about how to write ad copy for a bakery, and reading Aristotle and Quintilian may not seem at all practical.

But the skills you are learning in rhetoric are actually all about beauty, about expression, about learning to articulate clearly and communicate precisely in order that truth will seem desirable to the hearer.

It's about making that truth so utterly compelling that believing it is obligatory. And if, in the end, what you actually end up doing is becoming an entrepreneurial baker, hopefully your ability to communicate winsomely and effectively will ensure that you have the most successful bakery in the city.

CHAPTER EIGHT

Behind the Drill: Worldview Analysis

I hope that two things happened as you read that last chapter on rhetoric. First, I hope that you saw rhetoric as being potentially helpful in your future life—but I also actually hope that you had one or two objections beginning to form. If you and I had been in a face to face conversation while I said those things, I would really hope that you would be looking at me with a cynical expression on your face right now.

Did it occur to you that it may have sounded a bit like I was promoting sophistry? As if maybe I was insinuating that it would be a real win for your education if you were a horrible baker who churned out really lousy croissants—heavy and soggy and tough—but you could also trick rich people into investing their money, and you could fool customers into eating them, because you're just that persuasive? Like you could become an unscrupulous business owner or a weird cult leader, leading people astray by the sheer force of your impressive rhetoric?

To be honest, that's a real, live danger associated with the kind of education you're receiving, and it's a danger that I hope your parents are actively leaning against. To illustrate what I mean, I'm going to steal an analogy from my brother N.D. Wilson—and he used this analogy while talking to a room full of classical school teachers from around the country. Imagine a school where you took a whole bunch of kids, and from the time they were five years old until they were eighteen, your whole goal was to turn them into crazy special forces fighters. (Basically, picture a school where the entire school board and faculty was comprised of especially gnarly Spartans.) The students at this school learned weapons training and ninja skills and how to assassinate people in three easy steps. Let's further say you were successful, and these kids became an amazing and elite group—their test scores in "hand-to-hand fighting" and "sniper skills" and "leaving no evidence behind" were through the roof.

But let's also say that you forgot to teach them any loyalty. Or any concept of right and wrong. Or any three-step tests for when it's appropriate to use these skills and when it isn't. Or criteria for whom you should assassinate and whom you shouldn't.

Certainly we can see that kind of school would be horrific, and it would be very difficult to clean up the aftermath when (not if) it explodes. Similarly, the education you are receiving is geared towards turning you into a very effective, persuasive, powerful person—but if your education is neglecting to give you any sense of loyalty, or ethics, or discernment ... yikes. I hope you can see that the dangers, both to you and to society at large, would be enormous.

And that's why all of the "worldview" talk that you have to listen to all the time is not an irrelevant detail in your training. You've studied enough history and enough literature by now to realize that gifted, educated, persuasive people can change the world for good or for ill. Adolph Hitler, George Washington, Walt Whitman, George Whitfield, and Jean-Jacques Rousseau all set the world ablaze in one way or another.

"Changing the world" is not necessarily a positive thing in itself. Everything depends, obviously, on which direction that change is headed.

So yes, your parents want you to go out and change the world ... but not just in any old direction.

They want you to be anchored, to know who your people are, to fight for the right causes, to be wise, and to leave the world a better place than you found it.

They don't (I hope!) just want to see you get into a fancy-pants college with impressive scholarships. They don't just want to see you make piles of money and take expensive vacations or perform amazingly well on standardized tests. I hope your homeschool co-op isn't measuring its success based on how many of you get into the Ivy League or become lawyers or doctors. They want something much, much bigger than that. They want to see you go out into the world with your loyalties intact; they want to see you stand for the right things, and fight for the right things, and persuade others of the right things, everywhere you go throughout your life. They want to see you "enchant the souls" of all who come into contact with you as you display the beauty of the gospel in a full-orbed and robust Christian worldview. They want you to know what you think and why you think it and be able to winsomely explain it to others. They want to see you leave a mark on the world.

So, *worldview*. I hope you hear that word so often that you think it might be overkill. I hope you hear it in your Bible classes and in your lit classes and in your rhetoric classes and in your math classes and in your history classes—because that's what a world-

view is. It's a cohesive picture of all of life—seeing everything connect with everything else and being able to explain how each piece fits into the bigger picture. But it's not just about memorizing a bunch of magical propositional truths which, once you learn them, become the key to all other knowledge.

It is about seeing all of life—whatever you undertake and wherever you work—as connected in Christ and governed by Him.

If you think of logic and Latin as putting a sharp edge on your blade, and literature and rhetoric as giving you the skills necessary to fight effectively, then all the worldview training is pointing you in the right direction and helping you figure out who are allies and who are enemies and how and when you should fight which people. An understanding of the Christian worldview is by far the most important thing your school can give you—because a not-so-talented soldier who earned a C- in everything, fighting for the right side, is far to be preferred over a super ruthless and gifted general fighting for the wrong side.

So if your eyes glaze over whenever your teacher starts talking about the worldview of the poet you're studying, or you tune out whenever the class starts discussing pop culture and its implications, then I hope you also are bombing in logic and rhetoric and Latin as well. Because, and I acknowledge this cheerfully, if you graduate with all of the skills but none of the discernment, then you're actually turning into a monster.

CHAPTER NINE

Behind the Drill: The Maths & All That

It may seem more intuitive to you to learn math and science, because the world in general tends to see these classes as non-negotiables if you want to get a nice high-paying job in any of the STEM fields (science, technology, engineering, and math). And, of all your classes, these probably seem the closest to what the rest of the American kids are receiving, so it's possible you've never thought about how different what you are learning actually is. I mean, algebra is algebra, and $E= mc^2$ no matter what kind of class you learned it in, right? Well, it's not quite that simple.

In the math department, there is actually a substantial difference between you and the public school kids. In this case, it's not so much in what you're being taught as in how you're being taught to look at it. It's not as though you're learning different equations than the public school kids, or that the interior angles of triangles add up to 114 degrees over there in those schools. Those are things that are obviously the same no matter what. However, you are being taught that the world functions according to strict, predictable, constant, mathematical rules because God made it that way, and it's an expression of His character and goodness—and meanwhile the public schools are busily teaching that this math thing just sort of happened after a lot of gases randomly exploded and stuff sort of settled into a routine. (I'm not exaggerating.) This difference of perspective doesn't really change how the math works, but it does fundamentally change how you view it. For example, if you were walking through Florence, Italy and happened across Michelangelo's *David*, you wouldn't say to your friend, "Wow! Check out that rock! It looks just like a guy! How weird—I wonder where they found that!" You would actually stop and marvel at the artistry. If you found a wonky rock in the driveway that looked a little bit like a sheep, your reaction to it would be quite different—

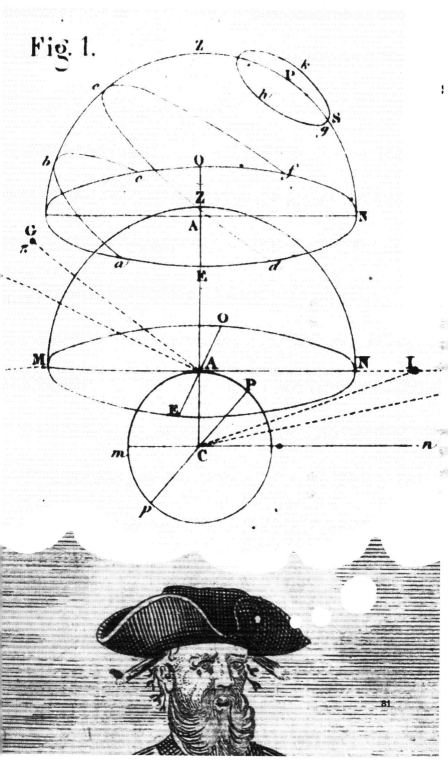

Fig. 1.

81

you would potentially marvel at the flukiness of it all, but you wouldn't stop to ponder the craft. **If you study math and see it as a reflection of your Creator—as the work of an artist with love and intentionality behind it—then you view math completely differently than someone who believes everything we see is the result of blind chance.** And although that doesn't change the mathematical formulae, it *does* change what you expect to find when you study the subject further and get into advanced physics or the philosophy of mathematics, to give two examples. Finding what you expect to find and the philosophy of mathematics are huge topics for another time, but suffice it to say that even in math classes, your educational perspective on the discipline is different!

That difference of perspective carries over into the sciences as well. If you believe in a creator God who spoke the universe into existence through the power of His Word, that changes absolutely everything. It changes how you study astronomy and biology and geology, because you are studying art—you're not just doing a survey of all the random and surprising but ultimately pointless things that carbon can turn into if you give it enough time. It is obviously impossible to work out all the many implications of this enormous subject here, even if this little book were much, much bigger than it actually is. But the presence of the Creator changes how you look at all the sciences—and when you change how you approach something, it affects what you discover there. If you look at creation as a *creation*, it changes the whole picture.

When we Christians look at the universe, we see a beautiful world that was given into our charge. Mankind was told to take dominion of it, and it was a good world that we were given to subdue. Then we broke it. Rather than taking dominion of it, we smashed it with our sin. We brought death and pain and suffering. We brought weeds and chaos into a world that now fights back against our attempts to cultivate it. If you take the truth that you learned in your morning doctrine class about the fall of man, and you bring that truth with you into your afternoon science class (rather than leaving it shut up inside your doctrine notebook), you will discover a profound intersection. If you read the account of the flood in Genesis and bring that with you into geology class, you suddenly won't simply be seeing sedimentary rock layers, you will also be seeing a story.

You'll be looking at the scars left by a flood, which was brought about by God's judgment for the profound sinfulness of man.

Our job as humans is still to take dominion—but dominion now looks like picking up the shattered pieces and working to restore something that has been broken. We can still see the artistry, but we also know that all of creation groans, waiting for redemption. When you study science like a Christian, you are learning more about the world which God created and commanded us to govern and subdue and restore—and that is a completely different perspective from what the secular scientists think they're doing.

The secular narrative and the Christian narrative are fundamentally at odds with each other, and this means that although we will agree on some things (the boiling temperature of water at sea level, for instance), we will interpret an awful lot of other things differently. We will look at geology and see in it evidence of what God has told us about the history of the world—while they, on the other hand, will look at it and insist it is evidence of a totally different story. Remember the analogy of the puzzle box? We look at the data around us and work to fit it together based on the picture that God gave us in His Word. The secularists insist that the pieces in front of us are supposed to make a completely different picture—one that they have figured out without any help from any stupid box. And, in case you were hoping we could all just get along, those people (especially in the STEM categories) are not okay with your Christian hypotheses.

All of us, Christians and non–Christians together, are staring at the same puzzle pieces, the same bits of data—but oftentimes we totally disagree on where the pieces fit. Frequently, God's revealed Word blatantly contradicts what all the guys with white lab coats and clipboards are telling you, and your parents are very likely having you learn all sorts of things in your science classes that would get snorted at in the public schools and state universities. I truly hope that they are also doing a good job of explaining to you why that doesn't matter in the least little bit. We believe in the infallibility of God's Word, and the secular educational establishment believes in the for-the-most-part-infallibility of science—but I'm afraid the track record of science isn't very infallible. It doesn't take very much work to come up with quite the list of things that "science" has claimed down through the centuries—things which, at the time, would get you absolutely ridiculed if you didn't believe ... and then, lo! It turned out that someone found new evidence, and science had to walk it back a little bit (or a lot, in most cases). Of course it was never the facts that changed, but rather the interpretation or understanding of them.

"Science" (or the scientific method) in the abstract is actually quite reliable, because it functions in the world that God made. The real margin of error comes down to the "scientists." Scientists have told us at various times that the earth is the center of the solar system, and that space is full of ether. Scientists have told us that you could turn lead into gold. Scientists scoffed their heads off about the idea of germs. Scientists have told us that sticking leeches on a sick person is a really hot idea. And when the scientists pronounce on these kinds of hypotheses, they frequently do it with all the authority of a priest delivering the truth from on high. This can sometimes feel very intimidating to Christians, and make us worry that our Bibles might be a bit outdated. But one extremely pertinent and oft-quoted truism is that he who marries the science of today will be a widow tomorrow. We, thankfully, serve a God who is the same yesterday, today, and forever. Cutting-edge theories may wither and the scientists fade, but the Word of the Lord endures forever.

That doesn't mean, of course, that science is a worthless pursuit. We are supposed to study creation—it's the glory of kings to search out a matter. We are supposed to dig and discover and invent and build and test and hypothesize and be wrong and learn more and try again—that's all part of what it means to be human, to be made in God's image, and to take dominion of this earth.

But we must always do it with an attitude of submission to God and His Word, testing all of our hypotheses against what He has told us—and that is the most fundamental difference between how you are being taught to study science and how the secular establishment wants to study science.

CHAPTER TEN

Behind the Drill: History

What about history, though? Surely we can all agree that history is the same no matter where you learn it, right? Facts, dates, names of generals, maps with little arrows indicating immigration patterns, tedious facts about principle exports—essentially just lots of things you try to forget as soon as humanly possible?

Well, first, I sincerely hope that's not what your history class is actually like, but I've also been around high school students enough in my life to know that this could easily be a student's synopsis of what history class is like.

Why do we study history, anyway? Maybe you are the student who really can't stand history, and it all seems super dull and pointless. If you were asked why you had to learn it, you might be genuinely stumped, because as you memorize facts about the ancient Assyrians, you feel like you're being forced to perform an utterly meaningless exercise. On the other hand, you could be a student who is super interested in history, and you love learning about World War II, and you probably enjoy watching documentaries on the History Channel in your free time. You don't resent history class because you are naturally predisposed to enjoy it. Even so, do you actually know why it's important—more than just "fun" to learn?

My guess is that the go-to answer to this question would be some form of the oft-quoted, "Those who forget the past are bound to repeat it." That's nice and catchy and seems both somewhat profound and also quite true. And it is. It's a good answer. **But by itself, it's not really enough to justify years of study. I mean, it's not like you might be tempted (in your thirties sometime) to fall into the Peloponnesian War, but luckily you had studied it in high school and were thus able to avoid it. Phew! Close call!**

So what does that phrase really mean? What really is the goal of teaching students history? First, let's lurch wildly off the expected path and ask—have you ever gotten lost in a mall? One of those mongo huge ones, and you get all turned around and can't find your way back to the department store where you parked? And you just seem to keep going by the Apple Store over and over, and you can't figure out why? In those situations, of course, you immediately start hunting around for those handy maps that they post periodically for the weary and the lost. The whole mall is neatly mapped out with a handy "You are here" clearly marked. Once you've found that map you're home free, right? You can look at where you're standing, find the destination you're trying to reach, and plan a route that does not involve going past the Apple store again. You might also notice why you had gotten caught up in that whirling eddy in the first place—what you had thought was a four-sided square was actually a trapezoid with other spokes off the corners, and that's why you kept getting mixed up. Or whatever. But the point is that you suddenly see everything much more clearly.

Now hold that image in your mind as you think about history. Here we all are, standing in America in the early-to-middle-ish part of the twenty-first century. How did we get here? In a hundred years, school children will be learning about our current events as historical events. The things which are sliding past us right now on our Facebook feeds will be their historical facts (well, some of them, at least). They'll be hearing summaries of our cultural issues and how we handled them. How *we* face and confront the challenges of our situation right now determines what *future* high school history tests will look like.

We're currently having fights about transgendered bathrooms, but why? Where on earth did that come from? Christian bakers are getting in trouble and having their businesses shut down because they refused to bake a cake for a gay wedding. But this wasn't a problem in the '50s. Why is it suddenly a problem now? Did these issues just arrive out of the blue? And what are we supposed to do about the situation now that we're actually here? Is there any way of putting this thing in reverse? Maybe someone can start with finding the brakes? How could we turn this thing around?

This is where we need to find a map.

We're standing here in a place we really shouldn't be—where did we take a wrong turn? And before we can figure out how to get out, we need to figure out how we got here in the first place. Was it when we turned right at the Cinnabon instead of left? Or was it much earlier than that? Do we need to retrace our steps all the way back to the Banana Republic?

Now, obviously, this analogy fails badly because history is far more tangled, far more nuanced, and frequently far more obscure than the nice tidy map of

a mall with straight lines. And plus, most of the time, we weren't the ones taking the wrong turn in the first place—it was actually our ancestors who, twenty or two hundred years ago, took the wrong turn. And then about 412 wrong turns after that. Sometimes we have to do a ton of work to even be able to read the map at all, sometimes the map is completely missing, and sometimes going back to the Banana Republic isn't even an option (!) because it got destroyed by the Ninevites and there's nothing left of it. (Yes, the metaphor has gotten out of control at this point.)

So, it's certainly not an easy thing to glibly point the way forth from the midst of all our current madness. But someone has to figure it out, right? Randomly charging down corridors does not generally yield good fruit and has never been shown to be an effective strategy (even in a mall). Someone really needs to learn to read maps and connect dots.

Actually, lots of someones need to do that. Thus, history class. So for example, take something that is very relevant to our current political discourse right now—say, abortion debates. What group historically lobbied for and demanded legalized abortion? Obviously, the feminists. And where did they come from? What caused them to spring up? How did the early feminist movement (demanding the right to vote) morph into the modern feminist movement (demanding lots of things including abortions)? How was the early feminist movement connected to the Civil War?

How was it a result of the state of the church at the time? And how did the state of the church at the time connect to the Second Great Awakening? And how did that connect to the War for Independence and the First Great Awakening? And how was the War for Independence an outgrowth of the Protestant Reformation? And at what point or points in that lineup did things go wrong? Finally, how can we answer those questions without being stupidly simplistic? Similarly, how can we address our current abortion question without circling straight into an earlier error which has already been tried and turned out to be ineffective?

The goal of studying history is not simply to exercise your memorizing muscle, pooling up historical facts the same way you might memorize the birthdates of all the players in the NFL—perhaps impressive but ultimately pointless.

The point of history is to teach you to be like the men of Issachar "who had understanding of the times, to know what Israel ought to do" (1 Chron. 12:32). And the reason history is so important is that we are actually all characters in a story. What happens in chapter 13 is intricately connected to the things that happened in chapters 1–12.

Obviously, you're not going to master every detail of history. That's much too big a job for anyone. And you're not going to remember each and every little thing you learn. But hopefully you'll come away from your years of history having a very basic and generally clear map in your head, beginning with the Garden of Eden and working its way down to twenty-first-century America. You'll know how the empires fit together. You'll know whom the Persians conquered and who conquered the Persians, and how that sets the stage for which parts of the Old Testament. You'll know where the greatest minds of history popped up on that basic timeline. And, importantly, you'll also know how to dig and find out more. You'll know how to ask the right questions, and you'll know that cultural phenomena never just arise out of thin air. You'll know how to begin to trace the thread back to something earlier, and how to identify causes and effects where other people only see chaos.

And, ultimately, this sort of wisdom will help you navigate all the decisions of your daily life: the little mundane things like which Tweets you click "like" on, and which political candidates you decide to support, and how you process the evening news.

CHAPTER ELEVEN

Complications with the Trivium

Up to this point we have been discussing specific classes that are different than what the average American student is getting. We've talked about Latin, which is obviously different, we've talked about literature and math and science and how you're getting a different take on those than most, we covered logic and rhetoric which most other teens are never taught, and we've talked about how the worldview training that permeates all of your classes is actually the most important piece of all. But some of this may be a bit confusing because you may have heard the terms "logic stage" or "rhetoric stage" thrown around, and that probably sounded like something completely different than what I've been talking about. And it is different actually, because those terms are about classical education theory, not just specific subjects. So let's thrash that part out.

In order to do this I'm going to have to give you a bit of a history lesson, some of which may be familiar to you. Bear with me.

You can't have hung around in classical education circles for as long as you have without hearing the word "trivium" bandied about, and you may already know that the trivium refers to the three disciplines of grammar, logic, and rhetoric. There's a lot of interesting stuff about the ancient Greeks and the Middle Ages and whatnot, but I'm not going to get into that. Suffice it to say, historically the seven liberal arts were made up of the trivium (the three aforementioned subjects) and the quadrivium (four more subjects—but I didn't need to tell you that did I, because I'm sure that, with your strong Latin instincts, you had already surmised it had four subjects). Anyway, the trivium was the foundation, and the quadrivium came second. Within the trivium, grammar meant the study of lots of facts, logic was the processing of those facts, and rhetoric was the winsome, persuasive application of the previous two. Notice that we are still talking about the actual subjects or disciplines. You have no doubt taken grammar class-

THE
SEVEN
LIBERAL
ARTS

TRIVIUM

GRAMMAR

LOGIC

RHETORIC

QUADRIVIUM

ARITHMETIC

GEOMETRY

MUSIC

ASTRONOMY

es and logic classes, and if you haven't taken rhetoric classes yet, you will. That is the logic and the rhetoric that I have been discussing in this book.

Skipping, skipping, skipping, we come to 1947. Enter Dorothy Sayers, an Oxford-educated English woman who wrote murder mysteries and was friends with Tolkien and Lewis. She wrote an essay titled "The Lost Tools of Learning" in which she lamented the loss of the older methods of education but also suggested something quite novel. She noticed that the three subjects of grammar, logic, and rhetoric also correspond with the natural stages of development from small children through adulthood. She observed that small children naturally love reciting facts—they're already in the phase of life in which they are having to learn new words and songs for everything anyway. So, she said, why not cut with the grain and stuff them full of facts and chants and songs? Their brains are sticky, they love to memorize, they love to recite. It makes sense to teach them "grammar-style" facts when they are naturally disposed to want to memorize them. She further observed that junior-high-aged students tend to be naturally argumentative—why not teach them logic (dialectic) during this "pert" phase? If they're going to argue anyway, why not teach them to do it correctly? She also noticed that the high-school-aged students are moving out of the pert stage and are becoming more attuned to beauty, art, poetry, and care more about expressing themselves well. This seems to be the natural age to teach rhetoric. I'm sure you can see the sense of this approach—imagine how successful it would be to try to teach winsome rhetoric to a bunch of ten-to-twelve-year-olds.

Fast forward even further. In 1981 a Christian school was starting in Moscow, Idaho, of all places, and one of the founding board members, Douglas Wilson, remembered having read Dorothy Sayers's essay back when he was a submariner in the Navy. The new school decided to go ahead and try out her theory, and the board structured their curriculum around this idea of dividing the three "subjects" of the trivium into three phases centered around elementary, junior high, and high school. That school opened in 1981 with eighteen students, and yours truly was in that kindergarten class because Douglas Wilson just happens to be my dad. And you know what? It worked! It turned out that Dorothy Sayers was really on to something. The whole approach was basically a giant experiment in raising the educational bar while at the same time also letting students learn what they're wired to learn at their current developmental stage. But the founders didn't just want to raise the bar educationally—they also wanted to turn out students who had a coherent worldview and who understood everything in the light of the Scriptures. Thus the classical and Christian educational movement was born.

This is all somewhat humorous, because in her

essay Dorothy Sayers remarks that "it is in the highest degree improbable that the reforms I propose will ever be carried into effect."

And yet—here you are.

Seventy years after Dorothy Sayers thought no one would ever try her idea, you are one of tens of thousands of students around the world sitting in classical homeschools and receiving an education that is both innovative and rooted in long tradition.

Talent in Real Life

Here's where I dish up what may possibly be bad news. Up until now I've been telling you about all the awesome things that you've been given, and so up until this point it's all fun and games really. But blessings always come with attendant duties, and I am going to absolutely refrain from cheesily saying that with great power comes great responsibility.

The fact that you are in the school you are in means that you have been given a giant, ridiculous, absurd blessing.

Remember at the beginning I talked about how you probably didn't choose this educational method yourself?

That it's simply being done to you? Well that's true on an earthly level—your parents are probably the ones who picked where to send you off to kindergarten—but it's also true that, **of all the places God could have had you live, this is where He picked.** He plunked you down in the middle of a huge blessing. You may already realize that, you may realize it later, or it's always possible that you could shut your eyes and refuse to ever acknowledge it at all—but it is true nonetheless. And Christ has words for people who have been given much—"To whom much is given, much is required."

Remember the parable of the talents in which the master gave one of his servants five talents, one of them two talents, and one of them one talent? This is actually quite a surprising story once you think about it, and if anyone but Jesus had told it, I think we would all be inclined to object to it as rather unfair. I'm sure you're familiar with the story, but let's refresh anyway.

The master left money with three of his servants and went away on a journey. The servants were expected to take the money and turn a profit on it. It was actually worth quite a lot—a "talent" was the largest unit of money in New Testament times and probably weighed about 75 pounds. That means a talent of silver could be worth a good $15K by today's standards.

(Obviously there are a lot of other factors that go into determining what the relative price is today—but my point is, the amounts in the story are much, much larger than your little sister's weekly allowance.)

So, two of the servants went and traded with that money (which does seem a bit risky, actually), and when the master came back, they returned the original money to him along with the extra they had earned. They did very well: the servant with five talents had earned an extra five, the servant with two had doubled his investment as well. And when they returned the money, they were rewarded by the master with a "well done good and faithful servant—enter into the joy of your master"—plus they were given even more responsibility.

But of course the third servant took what he had been given and buried it. Not only did he not trade with it, he didn't even invest it in a bank where it could have earned a bit of interest during the master's absence. Notice, though, that he didn't lose it or steal it—he was keeping it safe, right? But when the master returned and the servant dug his talent back up out of the back yard and returned it to him, he was straight-up rebuked! He returned the money when asked, but there was nothing extra to show for it. That servant was called wicked and slothful (doesn't that strike us as a bit harsh?), his talent was taken from him and given to the one with ten talents already (surely that's not very fair?), and Christ finishes the story by saying that servant will be cast into the outer darkness where there is weeping and gnashing of teeth. (Wow.)

So what's the point of that story? Jesus is telling us that our blessings have been given to us to use, not to bury. We're supposed to turn a profit, and we do this by investing the very blessing itself.

Lest you miss the point I'm trying to make, we are the servant in the story who has been given five talents. Some kids out there are given one talent, and they have to answer to God for it—but that's not us. I've spent this whole book showing classical Christian kids how we are being given more talents than most other Americans. And that comes with a heap of responsibility. God has entrusted us with something impressive, and we are expected to turn a profit on it. Some students graduate and leave homes like yours and absolutely excel. They stand on the shoulders of their parents and their instructors, and they make the most of what they've been given. They take the skills, the knowledge, and the worldview they received, and they go out and leave a mark on the world in lots of different, faithful, creative ways. Those students will be told, "Well done, good and faithful servants." But there are other students who graduate, take everything they learned, chuck it into the junk drawer of their minds, slam it shut, and never think about it again. They are the ones who are burying their talent—and they will have much to answer for when the master asks to see what they did with the blessings he gave them.

Of course other students actively throw their talent away, something which, apparently, the third servant didn't even think of. These types of students have the "slothful" servant beat for creativity, but I'm not sure that counts for much with the master.

So, take what you've been given and invest it wisely.

God is the one who has given it to you, and He's the one who will want to see what you've done with it. This is both intimidating and exciting, because God *does* want to see what you do. And this is why it is absolutely vital that you understand just what it is that you've been given. You can't invest and build with what you don't even realize you possess.

Real life doesn't start in college. You're well into it already. The choices you're making right now are setting the course for where you'll be in five years, in ten, and in fifty.

You're in a time of huge potential right now, because the concrete isn't set yet. You're in the fabulous position of still being right at the front-end of your life with loads of possibilities in front of you. So take a good look around you and really look at what God has given you to invest—and then roll up your sleeves and determine to make the absolute most of it. Good luck!